THE
SALE
OF
SALES

THE
SALE
OF
SALES

PRANNAY G SHARMA

Sarvatra

An imprint of Manjul Publishing House

Sarvatra
An imprint of Manjul Publishing House

• 2nd Floor, Usha Preet Complex,
42 Malviya Nagar, Bhopal 462 003 – India
• C-16, Sector 3, Noida, Uttar Pradesh 201301 – India
Website: www.manjulindia.com

This edition first published in 2023

The Sale of Sales
Copyright © Prannay G Sharma, 2023

ISBN 978-93-5543-308-4

Printed and bound in India by Repro India Ltd.

Prannay G Sharma asserts the moral right to be
identified as the author of this book.

CONTENTS

PREFACE

The author of this book is an accomplished and acclaimed sales honcho. Over the years, the subject of sales has been written about in countless books, but his view on the topic is entirely different.

Being a passionate professional, he has been watching the disparity between ground-level sales and those behind closed doors. It is escalating at an alarming rate, and this has resulted in fear and negativity for those pursuing a career in sales, especially in the current generation. During the pandemic, the author had ample time to scrutinize his assessments from decades of experience in this field. A few questions in his mind motivated him to pen down his thoughts on this vast and most underestimated subject.

"How do you motivate youngsters to pursue a career in sales?"

"What is lacking in the current scenario?"

"Why should sales trainings become mandatory?"

"How can organizations increase their sales figures?"

These, along with many other pathbreaking, ground reality questions, form the fundamentals of this book. It is written from the heart of a born sales professional who has taken up the mission to BRING BACK THE LOST SHINE OF A SALES CAREER.

In this book, he has managed to cover every aspect of sales, including all the phases from the past to the current scenario. His sole aim in writing and publishing this book is that more professionals take up this career with vigorous enthusiasm and make it a sought-after career path.

ACKNOWLEDGMENTS

I am grateful to my family, friends, and associates who have supported me in this great sycophantic endeavor.

It would not have been possible to accomplish this feat without their unwavering dedication and belief in my efforts and my abilities.

Further I would like to make a mention of all those noteworthy people who have been my mentors and hand-holders in my sales career. It is due to their strategic guidance that I have been able to write various chapters that all flow together.

INTRODUCTION

I LIVE, EAT, AND BREATHE SALES.

My love for this field was an inborn attribute, but I managed to stick to it due to my confidence in my career choice. Since childhood, I wanted to become a sales professional, and despite numerous hurdles, I achieved tremendous success in my career.

But over the years, I felt the need to pen down this book and offer my own perspective on sales. There have been many negative and disturbing incidents which further motivated me to guide my compatriots and the current as well as future generations to become passionate sales honchos.

Our ancestors never felt the need to find business. They were born salesmen. But why do we find ourselves lacking in this attitude? This is covered in one of the chapters in this book.

The various physical and mental attributes have been covered in Chapter . Sales is not only about passion. It is also about body language and having confidence in the product you are selling.

Chapter talks about the toxicity in the current sales scenario, which has impacted both professionals and companies.

Chapter talks about the mentality of buyers. When we talk about sales, we forget the most important hero of sales – and that is the buyer. What is he thinking when buying something, and what is his perspective?

The objective is to provide a strategic framework for a fresh business sales strategy and to offer ground-related techniques. My ambition is to unravel all the mysteries of sales and make it approachable.

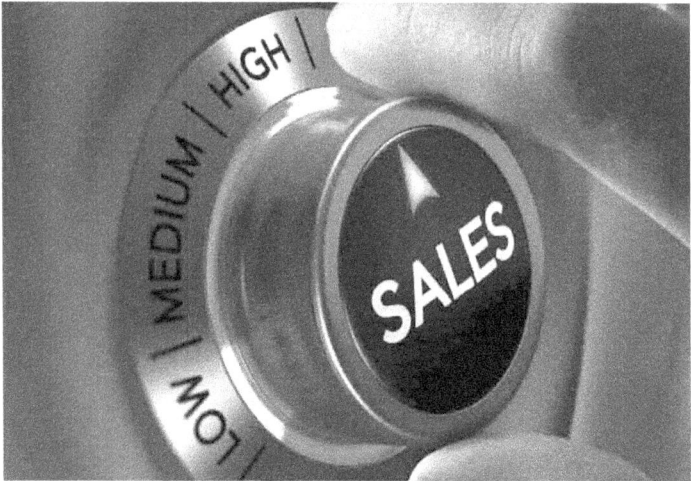

1

THE ANATOMY OF SALES

Since times immemorial, the field of sales has existed in numerous forms. Yesars ago, when people used the barter system (that is, exchange of products), it was also a form of a sale where instead of currency, people used to take food instead of something in their possession.

In the current scenario, too, sales are an integral part of every sphere and organization globally. But unlike other departments, it is based on the emotions and passions of the people involved. No amount of sales degrees or research on the subject is instrumental to the quantity of sales in a company. It is more about the matters of the heart and the zeal of the employees, which goes a long way toward acquiring deals and getting funds.

The fundamental principle of sales is purely selling an ethical and excellent-quality product. There is no place for inferior products or services, and the companies who adhere to these morals can be considered pure sales organizations. Mere exchange of products for money is done by even a street hawker. That is also a form of selling, and even huge organizations, and in fact every company, do sales in some form or the other. But are they ethical sales?

Sales is the most important division of every organization, because it is the core of revenue generation, on which the whole structure is based. Without selling, it is impossible for any business or organization to survive. But there are many factors associated with different regimes.

In the past few years, the purity of selling has diminished considerably. It has become almost mechanical, with scores of salespeople prancing in the field just trying to achieve their targets. This has resulted in frustration amongst buyers, who are now quite vigilant before they even think of purchasing anything. The trust factor is missing from sales because every employee just sees figures in their mind as they try to race to the top.

Join me, and let us retrieve the emotional and ethical essence of sales!

But prior to that, we need to explore the various forms of discrepancies and immoralities within sales which need to be removed entirely to create a new genre of clean and ethical selling.

> *"Do not focus on numbers. Focus on doing what you do best."*
>
> – Cassey Ho

"*The key to realizing a dream is to focus not on success but on significance – and then even the small steps and little victories along your path will take on greater meaning.*"

– Oprah Winfrey

2

THE PHYSICAL AND MENTAL ATTRIBUTES OF AN ACCOMPLISHED SALES HONCHO

In the olden days, there was a very common saying about salespeople.

"A man who can sell a comb to a bald man is the perfect sales professional."

The saying is quite simple, but it has infinite potential to help you understand the crux of sales. The current generation might laugh at it, but it is still true.

Why would a bald man buy a comb when he doesn't need one?

Well, there could be many ways to accomplish this sale. Although it seems impossible, it can be finalized. A bald man doesn't have hair, but his scalp might itch sometimes, so the comb could be used for that. He might not need the comb today, but he might after a few days, so that will motivate him to see his bright future when his hair grows back. Another way is to convince him that it is possible that when he uses it on his scalp daily, the blood vessels will become rejuvenated and the hair follicles will get a new lease on life.

So you can see that what seemed an impossible task (or a hilarious one) can be converted into a miraculous sales example, provided you pour your heart into it. So the main characteristic and outstanding attribute to have is to convince yourself that you can achieve it even if the customer doesn't need it. Your heart should beat for it, and your brain should conjecture about what would motivate the person to buy it even though he does not require it.

Even now, when you climb into a train or a bus, you will come across an endless stream of such innovative salespeople who will never accept failure. So, the most important lesson learned is to motivate buyers to understand why they need the product.

Nowadays, polished skills and fluent English combined with formal attire is mandatory for every salesperson. But what about body language?

"What physical attributes are necessary for perfect body language and to become a sales maestro?"

If you look closely at any accomplished sales employee, the first thing you'll notice is the confidence he has in his skills and the product.

Now where does that come from?

Some people are born with it, while some have to learn it. Before going for a sales meeting, you might be focused on your attire, but your optimism is what the buyer notices first.

If you are not confident of your product, how can the buyer be sure of purchasing it?

So, while a lot of information is imparted for products in every sales organization, your focus has to be more on your body language. It should exude the enthusiasm and confidence of a maestro.

CONCLUSION :

Sales is from the heart, by the heart, and for the heart. Just focus on doing sales with a focus on providing quality products and service, and your sales revenue will reach new heights.

> *"Become the person who would attract the results you seek."*
>
> – Jim Cathcart

> *"You're not obligated to win. You're obligated to keep trying to do the best you can every day."*
>
> – Marian Wright Edelman

3

SALES : MISUNDERSTOOD AND UNDERESTIMATED

Have you ever heard any parent having a conversation with their child about them entering into a career as a sales manager, a sales leader, or any other title associated with sales?

The answer of 90% of the people out there will definitely be a big NO. Why?

The simple answer is insecurity, inconsistency, and a bleak future. And in such a depressing scenario, when I myself thought about going into the sales field, I was ridiculed by all my family members. My love for sales and my enthusiasm were not enough to convince them, because they had seen salespeople suffering all kinds of humiliations not only in their companies but also from buyers. It was like I had committed a crime by thinking about it as a golden career.

Although my passion finally convinced them and I was able to achieve my ambition of becoming a flawless sales honcho, it made me think and introspect a lot. Why was there so much negativity for the main revenue churner of every organization?

When I dived deeply into this ocean of thoughts, I realized my experiences along this journey had also left me quite disturbed and ice cold. But the thrill and passion coursing through my veins have always managed to pull me back from the abyss and allow me to begin a new sales journey with renewed zeal.

I have eons of experience not only as a sales head but also as an entrepreneur, which has taught me many valuable lessons. From this medium, I wish to share them with my compatriots, peers, buyers, sellers, and, in fact, every individual, so that they value and respect the importance of selling.

It is an indispensable activity, and without ethical salespeople, the whole system will become rotten. Just like the heart of any human being, sales is the epicenter of the existence of every organization, and this is a bold move toward the revolution and pasteurization of sales.

CONCLUSION & SOLUTION

Introspection and retrospection are two important emotions attached to the improvement of sales. Just leaving any organization and joining a new one gives birth to a cycle of changes, which is endless.

A salesperson needs to introspect on the pros and cons before making any decision. There are flaws in every organization, but change is not the solution. The solution is bringing a solution for the negativities and overcoming them to reach the goal and the sales target.

Since sales is the revenue generation department, the responsibilities of sales employees should be their priority. They should not let minor incidents or grievances hamper their important contribution toward the survival of the organization.

Consider the bigger picture, and this is the best solution.

"Become the person who would attract the results you seek."

— Jim Cathcart

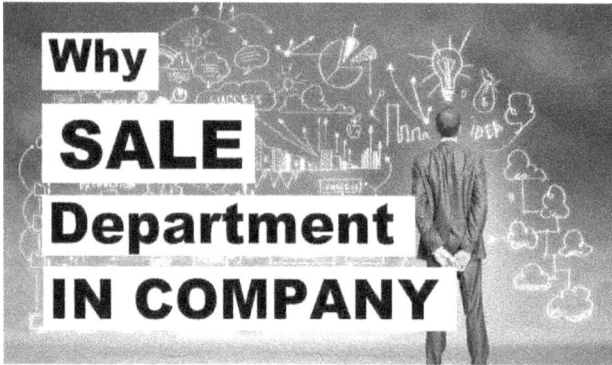

WHY SHOULD SALES BE THE PINNACLE OF CAREER CHOICES?

Although lakhs of people will argue that it is the most insecure, stressful and demeaning career, selling is heaven if done right.

There are hidden treasures besides the euphoria of selling and closing leads. The rewarding skills a salesperson develops, the people they encounter, and the various new lessons they learn besides the wads of currency are way above the hurdles in this profession.

REWARDING PLATFORM: SALES

A sales career is a platform to become the most outstanding professional, alongside funds way above those earned by others. The incentives which companies offer are sources of motivation and inspiration.

SURVIVAL SKILLS : OPTIMISM, ETC.

After going through the gruelling process of convincing customers, a salesperson develops the skills of survival in any situation or crisis. Thanks to their professional struggles, they develop the skills of handling and balancing.

In today's competitive world, physical and mental health are quite tough to sustain, but even with hectic work schedules, the passion of a salesperson keeps him alive.

> *"What differentiates sellers today is their ability to bring fresh ideas."*
>
> – Jill Konrath

IMPORTANCE OF SALES MANAGEMENT

> *"I have never worked a day in my life without selling. If I believe in something, I sell it, and I sell it hard."*
>
> – Estée Lauder

4

DESPERATE, DISTRESSED, AND DOOMED SALES

A few months ago, I met one of my college friends – my batchmate. While sitting in the cafeteria awaiting his arrival, I was looking at the flamboyant door with enthusiasm and palpitations. It had been years since we met, and the thought of hugging him again perked me up.

Suddenly, I felt a ghostly figure near my table. I felt goosebumps as I looked up excitedly. But all the euphoria vanished, and instead a feeling of gloom beset me and appalled me. My friend was a pale image of yesteryear, and his trademark infectious smile was gone.

"Hi. What happened? Are you okay?" A flurry of questions spilled from my mouth as his haggard figure slumped down on a chair near me.

He replied, "What can I tell you? For the past year, I have been in and out of many doctors' offices. But their diagnoses are not yielding any results. They say everything is fine, but I feel so tired and depressed. I have lost all the zeal in my life."

"Where are you working right now? What is your profile?"

He was aghast as he heard my questions. "You are more concerned with my work than with my health."

I just casually ordered our favorite coffee and looked up to him. "My friend, just answer my questions and I will give you the correct medicine."

"Well, I am working as a sales manager in a well-established company." He shrugged and answered my questions very nonchalantly.

I gave him a warm smile and whispered in his ear, "Your company and your seniors have the best treatment for you. Either talk to them, or just walk away. I took the same medicine six months ago, and I am now hale and hearty."

Although he pretended that everything was fine, the stress of achieving sales targets had been eating on his nerves for months. He was suffering from insomnia, which had resulted in various related problems. I could sense the doom, but why couldn't his seniors?

"Are sales targets so important that a human life seems immaterial?"

"Are salespeople doomed to be slaughtered like lambs?"

Unless there is an effort to transform the whole scenario and make it more warm, emotional, supportive, appealing, and optimistic, there are bound to be endless more patients like my friend.

"I have stood on a mountain of no's for one yes."
– B. Smith

The five out of ten calls you receive daily are from salespeople. What is the feeling you have when you reject those calls?

You reject their calls and are rude to them, but they still call. It is not like that they are robots without any feelings. They are desperate human beings hanging by the thread of sales. They want to close their targets however they can. They just want the buyer to say yes. They talk mechanically, speaking about their product for hours without even understanding what they are saying. It is just so distressing that most of them hang on to it just for their bread and butter and not for any kind of job satisfaction.

"Why are salespeople so desperate?"

"What kind of selling is that?"

It is not entirely their fault, but that of the entire system.

CONCLUSION AND SOLUTION

It is quite easy to point fingers at sales managers or sales heads and even executives for desperate or fraudulent sales. But where does that desperation to close leads come from?

The answer and solution is quite simple. It descends from the top to the bottom. The directors or CEOs need funds and revenue, for which they place the burden on their sales head, who in turn offloads it to his managers and executives.

"I want sales in any way possible. Today, you have to generate X in revenue."

This is a very common line heard in sales departments, and it resonates in the minds of the salespeople so much so that they just want to get funds at any cost. They compromise on their ethics and the happiness of their clients just to keep their seniors happy.

So, who is to be blamed?

We need to come together as a team. Every employee of a company needs to support the sales department. Whatever the issues are, they need to be resolved.

Before forcibly converting clients, seniors should ensure that the salespeople are relieved from the stress of working alone.

"Setting goals is the first step in turning the invisible into the visible."

— Tony Robbins

"Life shrinks or expands in proportion to one's courage."
— Anais Nin

5

HOW TO BECOME A
SALES EMPEROR

Sales is not a run-of-the-mill job where you have to follow a specific system. It is an exciting but simultaneously very competitive career wherein the salespeople need to be very passionate about their roles.

Your product will be the same, but it has to be sold with very ethical and strategic methods for different clients. Successful sales leaders are competitive, energetic, driven, passionate, communicative, inspiring, etc. Great sales leaders take these traits and combine them with their knowledge of the current sales scene as they integrate new technologies for modern selling. These leaders, who are ready to take on this challenge, are what high-growth startups need today.

STRATEGIC AND METHODICAL

In the current scenario, selling has become more focused on collection of leads. By following very simple yet focused strategies, the sales head can generate quality data for his team. Just the mere distribution of numbers or email IDs isn't productive. It needs to be collected according to the types of buyers required for the particular product or services of the organization.

Even top management needs to understand the importance of quality data and should not emphasize on closures from a collection of rubbish leads. There are scores of sources which can be helpful and productive and can be utilized for converting prospects into buyers. This needs careful analysis, from the top to the bottom. So, before you pounce on the targets, design an action plan for generating very productive and noteworthy leads.

INNOVATIVE AND STRATEGIC

It is very crucial to visualize the whole department as a family. In the olden days, and even now in some companies, there is no such thing as an individual portfolio. From the most senior member to the tiniest one, everyone is assigned duties, but if there are signs of failure then they come together as one unit to design new and innovative strategies for attaining the desired results.

It should not be an individual employee's target, but that of the entire organization. If, even after various attempts, sales are not happening, then rather than venting frustration on the team or leader, unique strategies should be designed for fruitful results. This needs quite a bit of brainstorming. Don't consider it a wastage of time, but a journey toward the goal.

FOCUSED LISTENING SKILLS

The most important skill any sales leader or even small sales employee can have is the ability to listen patiently. Modern sales leaders know how to listen. A true leader gives importance to the listening power of his team members. When a customer is expressing his requirements, a lot of patience is needed, but it is necessary in order to understand how to close the deal satisfactorily.

Clients relate with executives who listen more than they speak. The same is true for team members, so a true leader will always be patient enough to listen to what they wish to communicate.

DISTRIBUTION OF TASKS

An experienced sales head or leader understands the importance of walking together as a team. They assign specific tasks to each member of the team. Distributing the workload to the entire team allows them to focus on more important tasks.

But delegating isn't simply assigning random tasks to whoever's available. Good leaders know the strengths and skills of each team member. They designate certain tasks according to the abilities of each member of the team.

DECISION-TAKING SKILLS

Decisions in sales are not just taken out of the blue. They need the expertise and finesse which come with experience and knowledge of the intricacies of the field. The most important quality a sales leader or senior salesperson can have is his judgmental skill and firmness in taking decisions.

Before taking any decision, a sales leader has to take into consideration various factors because the implications of his decision will shape many destinies.

So, understanding and examining are mandatory skills. His team members will appreciate it if they find him relating to the events happening at the company. If he falters, the whole team spirals into doom.

DISCIPLINED AND SYSTEMATIC

It is not child's play to manage a large group of team members and get the work done from each individual. Sometimes, it can really get on one's nerves, but if a person is systematic and disciplined, they can really do wonders.

It can get overwhelming more often than expected, but a good sales leader never falls behind. They're always on top of everything. But don't expect them to have superpowers. They just know what needs to be done and put the tools at their disposal to good use.

PROFICIENT MOTIVATOR

It is not humanly possible to be successful every time, day in and day out. No matter how hard salespeople work and put in effort, they cannot always achieve the targets they set.

As a result, they fall prey to stress and anxiety, which sometimes results in sometimes serious ailments. That is the blunt truth – the sales portfolio is not for those who succumb to failures very easily. Very often, even the most strong and courageous people feel demotivated. During such moments, sales heads need to be very supportive and motivational and be pillars of strength for their teams.

TRAINER PSYCHOLOGY

It has been seen in many companies that the sales leaders have very restrained approaches toward their sales teams. They feel that training and teaching their juniors can create competitors, but there they are quite wrong. Leaders need to be very confident and secure.

Good leaders not only have the skills to give excellent coaching, but enjoy doing so. Manipulative and authoritative leaders assume their team members respond well to only their instructions.

This approach is too one-sided, and it doesn't foster a mutually beneficial relationship between the manager and direct report. It is more about developing each member of your team to take on increasing levels of responsibility.

They're not just managing people to be excellent sellers; they're also shaping them up to be future sales leaders.

AN EYE FOR SALES TALENT

Thanks to years of experience, sales leaders develop the intuition and skills necessary to catch the best and most talented salespeople. But it is very crucial to focus on their selling skills rather than their resume. Many times, companies hire a person for a senior sales position just on the basis of his magnanimous achievements, but later regret their decision. So, it is quite imperative to be sharp while hiring.

Even a fresher with less experience but loads of determination and the passion to succeed can become an excellent sales honcho. The only thing they need is effective guidance and a welcoming atmosphere.

CONCLUSION AND SOLUTION

An excellent sales leader and salesperson should be a combination of all the aforementioned characteristics. But it takes time and efforts to develop them and maintain them to achieve high productivity.

Learn from your superiors and peers who have the right qualities. Drop the ego and be a learner, and you will become a perfect sales achiever.

If considered a passion and not just a job, sales will take you to the heights of success.

Simultaneously, companies should also invest in training sessions and motivational seminars for every salesperson so that they don't lose their passion.

"A salesperson's ethics and values contribute more to sales success than do techniques or strategies."
— Ron Willingham

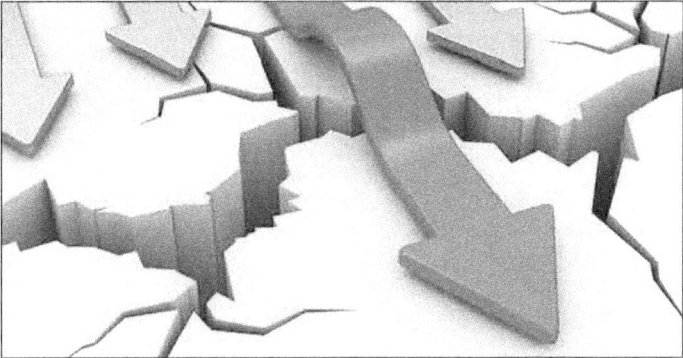

6

MANIPULATION IN SALES AND ITS REPERCUSSIONS

I just went to the hospital yesterday near my place to see a friend admitted there for surgery. While I was sitting in the waiting lounge, a piercing scream suddenly shook my heart. A family was crying inconsolably near a hospital stretcher. I felt the urge to approach them and console them but as I went near, I saw a very young man lying there motionless.

His mother spoke brokenly. "He was under so much pressure to perform that he went ahead and even manipulated his figures sometimes just to keep his bosses happy. We are very ethical people, and he couldn't face all the unethical practices being committed in his organization, wherein his boss was the one conniving along with the seniors. He just had a stroke from all the stress, and now he is gone."

"Pranay, this is our sales target. We have to achieve it at any cost." I could still hear my CEO shouting at me. I can very well understand the kind of stress and tension those words caused.

Almost every unethical manipulation technique was being used in the sales department, and even senior management was a part of it. The figures were just to see the spark of happiness in the clients' eyes and make the competitors jealous.

"What the hell was happening?" I used to shout out loud on reaching home but before the raging fire could burn me out, I shifted to another promising profile. If I hadn't, I would have landed on that stretcher, too. But inside my heart, I knew that someone had to clean up the mess of manipulation.

WHY NOT ME?

If the company meets its sales guidance, the company is rewarded and the stock price rises; if it fails to meet the guidance, the price is hammered. Very often, this motivates companies to manipulate their sales. In fact, sales, or the top line, is one of the easiest figures to manipulate with a number of techniques available.

So, what are these techniques? And is it possible to find out such companies through some early signs or red flags? Let's have a look.

The different techniques for manipulating sales

There are four different techniques available to companies :

1. Predicted financials
2. Fictitious revenue
3. Considering deals closed even if buyers' payment remains uncertain
4. Unsustainable activities

    Let us delve deeper.

1. Predicted financials

The most prevalent technique to manipulate sales is using predicted financial earnings as revenue generated. This is the most common technique that companies employ to manipulate sales, and the easiest way is to record revenue early when it clearly belongs to a future predicted date.

For example, a company made a 3-year contract but starts considering the future income as predicted revenue and includes it in the current financials or revenue generated.

2. Fictitious revenue

Making fake entries in the accounts and sales is a bigger crime than any other form of manipulation. The companies who resort to this kind of malpractice are under the impression that they can get away with such fake revenue. Well, most do, but ultimately, they are only cheating themselves.

Whom do you want to impress with fake revenue?

Your prospects, competitors, clients, employees? But finally, did you achieve what you wanted to?

First, let us understand how this is done.

There are 2 ways in which companies can record fictitious revenue.

Fake invoices – faking invoices is one of the easiest ways used by companies to inflate sales.

In the past few years, there have been lot of scams wherein fake invoices were the main methodology. Companies resort to such techniques to try to get away with manipulation.

Inflated invoices have now become very common, and this is a serious matter. The people handling financial matters create or procure such invoices which are completely fake, and this is sometimes done at the behest of the management itself.

Fake products – in order to show increased revenue, many companies resort to another technique: that is, to create fake products. It may sound quite unbelievable, but many companies have done that, and still do. Even some companies offering educational products and coaching resort to such manipulation. They charge fees for some products or services which exist solely on paper, and this results in the failure of the organization.

Indirect or interrelated dealings – in some companies, the revenue is fraudulently shown in the form of dealings with related parties, such as to a vendor, relative, consultant, broker, or business partner. While working with a few companies, I came across many such fake figures or bloated figures for dealings which were never done.

It seems quite easy to fake such figures, but in the long run, it raises suspicion if done frequently. If the sales are low or a product isn't being accepted in the market, then efforts should be undertaken to find the reasons and rectify the mistakes. Resorting to malpractice gives rise to cheating and trust issues within the company, too. Your clients and prospects will lose their faith in you once your secrets are out.

3. Adding figures to revenue when buyers' payment is uncertain

One of the most important things to look for is the ability of a company's customers to pay back the company.

Financial crunch or inability of buyers to pay – some educational products companies are selling their products to customers who don't have the resources, but still they consider them as sales.

Some real estate companies sell flats to customers whose financial resources are very low, but their salespeople are not bothered. They consider it as a sale while the buyer is not able to pay even the first instalment of the home loan. So don't go for such kind of doomed sales.

Extended or flexible payment terms – companies sometimes offer better or flexible payment terms in order to entice their customers to buy additional products and generate higher sales. While such arrangements definitely prop up revenue for the time being, they pose an increased risk of the payment never being realized!

UNETHICAL SALES GRAPH GROWTH

It might seem obnoxious, but companies sell their assets to overcome their losses. In some cases, construction companies even sell the same property to multiple buyers. Or sometimes only a few bungalows or flats have been sold, but the directors force the sales department to go ahead with sales even when they are not certain that the project will be completed.

Companies are usually in possession of several fixed assets used in the production of their goods and services.

At times, some of these fixed assets may be surplus to the requirement. Even though the assets have been pledged to banks, they are still sold discreetly.

And at times, the business might be in desperate need of cash and decide to sell some of its fixed assets. When inappropriately accounted for, these one-time gains can be used by companies to artificially boost revenue. Investors thus need to check these accounting entries thoroughly.

PROMINENT AND PUBLISHED EXAMPLES OF MANIPULATION AND MALPRACTICES

ARTICLE PUBLISHED BY DECCAN HERALD

Selling hope: Parents fall for ed-tech's false promises

https://www.deccanherald.com/specials/ insight/selling-hope-parents-fall-for-ed-techs-false-promises-1109289.html

This is one of the millions of examples of fraud sales and faking sales.

CONCLUSION AND SOLUTION

There is no shortcut to success. So rather than adopting manipulative techniques, try to motivate your salespeople to focus on closing deals. In case a product is not selling, the seniors and owners should find out the shortcomings. The focus of the company should be on improving the quality of the product and creating it as per the market standards so that the salespeople can sell them to buyers easily.

Fake products and fake dealings have a limited life and will come to an end one day. So be honest and transparent in all your dealings. It might take a longer period to grow, but it will be sustainable forever.

In the olden days, education was given free to students, and the norm was just giving Gurudakshina. Teaching students and shaping their career was considered to be a noble profession, but during the last few decades it has become just a money-making machine. It should be done as a business, but also place emphasis on the ethics and purity of sales to parents and students. Frauds in such companies shake the very core of education, and giving fake figures just to impress clients and investors should be avoided when creating a niche in the market. If you are imparting the right education through perfect means, then nothing can stop you from becoming successful.

Word of mouth is the best form of marketing and publicity.

Importance of ethics in SELLING

- Ethics are highly valued because:

  - Salespeople are the face of the company
  - Customer's evaluate the company's ethical standards
  - **Trust** is the foundation of relationships

"Just don't give up what you're trying to do. Where there is love and inspiration, I don't think you can go wrong."

– Ella Fitzgerald

7

THE TOXICITY
OF THE CURRENT SALES
CULTURE AND STRATEGIES
TO ABOLISH IT

A positive sales attitude attracts more customers and contributes to forging a relationship with them for the long haul. It has been proven numerous times that a sales team with a good sales culture incorporating a positive attitude, professional conduct, and discipline can give tremendous results for the business, and ultimately for all the stakeholders.

A salesperson's primary purpose is to make a sale and generate revenue for the business, thus contributing to achieving its goal. One of the biggest hindrances in doing this is an unfavorable work environment or a toxic work culture.

An organization should never endorse a toxic work culture. It is an immoral practice and has a negative impact on the overall well-being of the business. These toxic traits in the sales team culture are often dormant and may not surface much in day-to-day business dealings. Sometimes, the problem is noticed only after a devastating sales review.

SIGNS OF A TOXIC SALES CULTURE

"Prevention is better than a cure" – the proverb seems to stand true for everything of value. And the first step to prevent something is to identify the problem.

Here are some of the most common signs of a toxic workplace culture that lead to sales team attrition:

A) A very disturbing employee turnover

No one ever wants to work at a place that follows a toxic team culture. Sales is already a stressful job, and the responsibility of bringing in revenue is huge. If you discover random hiring and firing going on at your office or you find employees vanishing at a fast pace, then it could be a sign of a toxic work culture. If the company doesn't pay heed to the unfavorable work conditions, employees lose interest in the job and quit.

Be vigilant and do systematic analysis

B) Hazy transparency

In most companies, there is almost zero transparency and communication, which results in reaching the goal . When a person holding the information stops being transparent with others, they create an information gap that causes miscommunication. Transparency is very crucial for success in any personal or professional relationship. If you are always explaining yourself or facing delays communicating with your team, you should fix that problem soon.

C) The predator

Most top performers gradually become predators. They ridicule those who find it difficult to reach their targets, and this results in a toxic ambience. A salesperson's great performance shouldn't be an excuse for them to not be team players or act arbitrarily. Sometimes, the senior management also supports their toxicity due to their contributions to the revenue. This psychology causes dissatisfaction amongst the subordinates and creates a toxic environment. Especially so when you ignore bad habits and immorality to focus on higher sales figures.

D) Ignorance of irrational behavior

Ignorance of politics and misbehavior amongst the employees of an organization results in a very poisonous atmosphere. This type of behavior sometimes includes rubbish language and absurd comments about people, below-average sales performance, or reoccurring irresponsible behavior. Therefore, appropriate action should be taken to stop unacceptable conduct.

E) Assigning impossible targets

Impossible targets are demotivating. Companies often make the mistake of setting unattainable goals that are impractical and unrealistic. But when the sales team is given an impossible task, their morale takes a hit and it leaves them frustrated and unmotivated. This practice is quite common with pharma sales reps.

Strategies to improve sales culture and lighten a toxic work environment

The first step toward overcoming or improving a sales culture is identifying the problem and its root cause. Yours could be that your team is not communicating with each other, or that your manager is abusing their authority. Whatever your problem is, you first have to identify it and take some action to create a healthy sales culture for your organization. Here are some of the most effective ways to overcome such a culture:

A) Recruit the passionate and perfect

If a person having knowledge of the financial field is hired by an education company for their accounts or funding, then it is quite reasonable. But if he is hired for sales, he has to match the skills they need. Apply the right methods to find out if an applicant's expectations and skillsets match your requirements. For example, if you are looking for a sales rep to sell educational products, scrutinize candidates with extensive knowledge of the field.

B) Empathetic and supportive ambience

A supportive and empathetic ambience can work wonders in an organization. Employees spend the maximum time in the office, and if the ambiance is toxic, it will reflect in their personality and ultimately lead to disasters. A casual work environment is more productive and creative than a dictatorial workplace that doesn't allow any room for personal interactions.

C) Flow of honest communication

Like a waterfall, the communication system should be flawless, from the senior leaders to the person at the bottom end. Advantages of an open chain of communication include a greater level of trust amongst the team, transparency in day-to-day business and important notifications, immediate resolution of conflict or query, and room for innovation.

D) Distribution of responsibilities

When you give someone a task, you share responsibility, and when you do that, you should hold that person accountable for their responsibility. This creates a sense of motivation in the team to finish the task, as a sense of responsibility is attached. Additionally, a follow-up meeting to check up on tasks can help in keeping things on track.

E) Inspirational hand holding

Whenever there is an aura of failures and rejections, just have a small inspirational get-together with the employees and sales executives. An incentive for timely completion of work, overtime, extra commissions, and some one-on-one interaction with the employee can multiply their performance by a great extent. Another reason to motivate your team is that a leader who leads by example is more likely to follow others . Active involvement in motivating the team reflects your commitment to the business.

F) Systematic regular training sessions

Even the most experienced salespeople need training to understand the products which they need to sell. Sales is a game of skills, and to get the most out of your sales team, you need them to upgrade their skills. To do that, you can incorporate regular training in sales and related fields for the sales team. The positivity and confidence of salespeople is crucial because they represent the organization; they deal with the clients on the company's behalf.

G) Accept defeats

For decades, sales has been only winning and not losing. A sale is not always about finalizing a deal or closing a lead. It is about living people full of emotions. It is about getting customers and solving their problems.

Learn to accept failures and adapt according to the lessons they teach you. You will never commit the same mistake again. So, if a prospective client says no, it's not a loss because he can lead you to positive leads if you consider your relationship with him and not just think of him as a negative prospect. Rejections in sales are typical. It is a competitive world, and if you wish to achieve more significant goals for your business and sales team, let little failures be and take the lessons in stride.

CONCLUSION

A positive and nurturing sales environment is necessary for the employees and the business. A toxic one can lead to various issues and deteriorate the health of the business. It is evident now that no one likes to be employed at a place with a bad reputation.

Thus, finding measures to overcome these flaws and improve the work culture becomes essential for businesses. This improves sales team retention, builds a healthy work environment, and most importantly, results in a highly motivated sales team.

> "*There have been so many people who have said to me, 'You can't do that,' but I've had an innate belief that they were wrong. Be unwavering and relentless in your approach.*"
>
> – Halle Berry

HOW DO YOU HANDLE NEGATIVE SALESPEOPLE?

The solution: Being around a negative person can be toxic for the whole organization.

To handle this type of salesperson, **have a one-on-one session with them. Rather than ridiculing them, be very specific and empathetic in pointing out the incidents when their attitude or statements have become a cause for concern for the company.**

Also, listen to the reasons why they feel this way toward the company. Remember that your critics are your best friends because they always tell the truth about your blemishes. Just firing negative people is not the proper solution, because they will go to some other company and speak negatively about your company.

Even if they are let go, it should be done in a very cordial manner so that they leave all the resentment behind closed doors. Understand their feelings toward the company and the reasons behind the poisonous attitude, and if there is even one iota of truth within, rectify the issues as soon as possible.

WHAT ARE THE SIGNS OF A TOXIC COMPANY?

There are some very evident signs that your workplace culture is quite toxic and needs to be transformed:

Little to no enthusiasm in the employees.

A very strong fear of failure.

A constant aura of confusion.

Too much gossiping and arguments.

Frequent hiring and firing of sales employees.

CHARACTERISTICS A SALESPERSON SHOULD NOT POSSESS

Characteristics of a bad salesperson

While travelling on a bus or a local train, you must have encountered salespeople busy selling their wares. This practice has existed for decades and will never die, because they are the ultimate sales guys who never lose their exuberance.

Their characteristics are inborn and not learned from any training, so kindly defer from going into sales if any of the following apply to you :

- Lack of motivation to perform sales.
- Fear of rejection and inability to accept failures.
- Miniscule knowledge of the product and a lack of passion to acquire any more.
- Being inattentive or a bad listener.
- Lacking the ability to ask the right questions.
- Overconfidence and the belief that you do everything right.

- Lack of genuine social empathy.
- Focusing only on targets and not the desire of the customer, and trying to force them to buy your product to get sales.

CONCLUSION:

Shift your focus on people instead of products.

WHY DO PEOPLE NOT LIKE SALESPEOPLE?

In the '60s and '70s, a salesman was like family. He was welcomed and treated like others because there was no such thing as 'selling' by the salesman. It was pure exchange of products for money based on trust. Selling and buying only took a few minutes; the rest of the time was just maintaining relationships and improving bonds.

In the '90s and after, the focus was more on learning the evolving techniques, but since there was ethical selling, salesmen were still welcome.

In 2022, the moment a prospect picks a call and it is from a salesman, he utters a sigh of exasperation or frustration. When the doorbell rings and a salesperson is found at the door, people just bang the door shut without even looking at what he or she is selling.

You can't blame them. They are suffering from salesman syndrome: frantic calls, fake calls, and random calls at any hour of the day.

So then how can you expect people to like salespeople?

> *"I have never worked a day in my life without selling. If I believe in something, I sell it, and I sell it hard."*
>
> — Estée Lauder

PROMINENT SIGNS OF A TOXIC TEAM

A sales leader or manager can easily sense a toxic team if he carefully looks at their behavior. It is very obvious if the executives or team members are interested more in gossiping rather than working. Their negativity is poured in words.

Sometimes, they pretend to be working, but are more interested in pulling down others and even demeaning them in front of the leader. This leads to a very nail-biting competition rather than a healthy one, and rather than being about hitting the targets, it becomes more about insulting others and forcing them to quit the race.

SOLUTIONS

Build a network of trustworthy colleagues. Toxic workplaces are filled with people who are egoistic and manipulative.

1. Stay focused on important goals.
2. Be pleasant to everyone.
3. Create a beautiful work–life balance.
4. Situations are temporary.
5. Go for a healthier workplace.

"You can never leave footprints that last if you are always walking on tiptoe."

– Leymah Gbowee

HOW TO TELL IF A WORK ENVIRONMENT IS TOXIC

1. TURNOVER. The most obvious symptom of a toxic work environment is turnover.

2. A POISONOUS CULTURE.
3. STRUCTURAL FEAR OF RETRIBUTION.
4. GOSSIP.
5. TROUBLING BEHAVIORS OR BODY LANGUAGE.
6. NON-COMMUNICATIVE TEAM MEMBERS.
7. DISTRUST BETWEEN COLLEAGUES.
8. A LACK OF CONFIDENCE IN LEADERSHIP.

CONCLUSION

The HR department can play an important role in clearing the toxicity. Dealing neutrally with negative people should be the norm, rather than ridiculing and firing them.

WHY DON'T SALES MATERIALIZE?

It is quite obvious.

Harassment of customers is one of the main reasons. Take the example of some of the leading coaching institutions and insurance companies. Near each month's end, they repeatedly call clients and even resort to pathetic methods to try to convince them and close the sales.

Will such sales materialize?

This is not sales but clear manipulation, which has become very common.

Manipulation is about doing whatever you have to in order to get what you want. It's just as much about fooling people as it is about transparency and a positive attitude. Manipulate prospective customers by luring them into making sales with the content on your website.

For example, a customer or a parent who wants the best coaching from your educational institution should have the methodology and its benefits explained to them instead of you focusing on the packages first. Parents are concerned more about results, so listen to them patiently and satisfy their queries.

Don't brainwash them for the sake of closing a deal.

Don't slaughter them; rather, think about how you can pacify their concerns.

As a sales representative, your gut will tell you whether the customer is interested or not. Don't bore or confuse them with unnecessary information before you are even sure they are interested.

Also, observe how comfortable the client is with any technical words and the language being spoken. If he seems uncomfortable, then switch over to his preferred language and make the pitch very simple. Every client is different, so understand their perspective first.

BE VERY OBSERVANT OF COMPETITORS

In some companies, the sales leaders send their own team members to their competitors as clients to understand their strategies. This might be considered a healthy norm if you just observe and adapt any positive practices.

But if the sales executives or managers are forced to trap the clients of competitors, then it is clearly a form of cheating, and these kinds of sales will never materialize.

Rather than cheating, just prepare new, more competitive strategies which give a boost to sales. If the management follows fair practices while keeping an eye on their competitors, then there will surely be a growth in sales.

TIME TO BOW DOWN AND QUIT

Sometimes, due to pressure to achieve targets, salespeople keep on ranting and making speeches without even thinking rationally. It is not humanly possible to be a success all the time. No matter how hard you try, even the best prospects will fail to comply.

Just like a true warrior, it is very important to acknowledge and accept your failures, and this is a very important part of your sales strategy.

Clients and investors recognize and relate to you as the face of the organization, and this makes you a very prominent figure. If you commit any mistakes or behave irrationally, ultimately, you are tarnishing the image of the company. Don't push the prospects so far that they retaliate and behave aggressively. Rather, bow down and accept what they are trying to communicate to you. They will come back to you whenever they are comfortable.

To quit doesn't mean that your strategies have failed; rather, it is an eye-opener for you and the company that helps you identify the reasons and rectify the faults. Don't spend your energy and time on dealing with the people who don't have the authority to take decisions. It will demotivate you, so quit and proceed to the next one.

Don't manipulate; rather, find out some outstanding strategies to reach your goal. Make use of some of the methodologies and see your company prosper.

You May Be Committing Sales Malpractice If You're...

8

TOXIC BOSSES AND
HOW TO HANDLE THEM

INSECURE BOSSES:

2 THINGS INSECURE BOSSES DO

1. Only hire candidates less capable than themselves

2. Withholding information to become indispensable

The moment you walk inside the office, you can sense the negativity in the ambience. Sometimes, the insecurity is quite evident, but there are also tell-tale signs which can really make a sales employee gradually realize where he has landed.

In most cases, an insecure boss is the first one to take the benefit of your hard work and very shamelessly do it in front of you.

They effortlessly accept appreciation for work done by you.

They're always restraining you from meeting other colleagues and advancing.

They try to be in total control of you everywhere.

They get aggressive without any valid reason.

They're so hands-off you forget they're there.

HOW DO YOU DEAL WITH AN INSECURE BOSS?

It is quite claustrophobic to work with an insecure and nerve-wracking boss, but leaving the job is a cowardly solution. In sales specifically, the number of such kinds of bosses is very high – perhaps because of the stressful atmosphere.

So what should your approach be?

WHY DOES A BOSS FEEL INSECURE?

Perhaps because he thinks you are more capable than him and might be the one to take his position in case he fails to accomplish the expectations of revenue generation.

In some cases, they are not as confident as they seem to be and so they try to demean their juniors to show their superiority. I myself have been the victim of such obscure psychological crimes. In some cases, I left with a heavy heart and joined another company, but then it seemed endless and I was the one who was suffering it all, both personally and professionally.

Finally, I decided that I had to take a stand and not let it get on my nerves but it still continued. Whenever I used to approach my boss for my work, he used to give me the cold shoulder. Although he had been in the organization for many years, my knowledge and experience made him nervous, and he used to lose control without any specific reason.

It was quite frightening initially, but after I gave it a thought and worked it out systematically, I gathered the courage to face him without feeling suffocated.

So, the best strategy is to support him and let him feel that his position is not in any danger. Try to coax him to share his experiences and make him feel comfortable in your company. That will make him much more amiable, and once it happens, be honest and transparent about your sufferings. If he understands, he will change, but if he doesn't, then you need to approach senior management before you think of leaving, because they have the authority to stop this kind of harassment.

"Having a bad boss isn't your fault. Staying with one is."
— Nora Denzel

2) Insecure interviewer

I remember one special day when I was preparing to

interview for a senior sales position at a reputed company. Although I was a little nervous, my experience and skills gave me the confidence that I could bag the position. More than myself, my friends and past associates were optimistic because they knew my skills and had seen my performance. But I was in for a rude shock.

As soon as the interview started, I somehow felt that it was not going the right way. The interviewer was quite edgy and just seemed interested in finishing it off without even asking the relevant questions. It felt quite strange, but I couldn't fathom the reason.

I called up my friend while quite dejected and in an emotional state and gave him the complete, detailed sequence of events. Although he was quite taken aback, he consoled me with a simple answer: "The interviewer was insecure because he knew that if you were selected his, position would be in danger. But it is actually the misfortune of the company because they lost a talented person like you due to the insecurity and selfishness of their senior sales employee. The politics in the sales department results in grave losses to an organization."

Hearing this, I felt the pain in my heart replaced by a sense of loss and despair. It was a gloomy feeling – less for my loss and more for the organization where such kind of treatment resulted in the loss of deserving candidates and revenue. But there must be millions like me feeling dejected because they didn't know the real reason for their rejection.

Companies don't realize this mismanagement in the sales department and the blunders of their salespeople and other seniors but when they do it is already too late to rectify.

Due to the sheer selfishness and insecurity of an employee, they lose sincere, efficient, productive sales executives and experienced senior people who could have taken the company to the heights of success. But most of them are not even aware or bothered about what is happening under their nose. They are just so focused on revenue generation that they simply choose to look away and brush every problem under the carpet.

When such companies suffer revenue losses and are declared a failure, then whom do they blame? They definitely blame their sales team and the other employees, but they fail to find and put down the fire that generated the havoc.

SOLUTION

The solution to this pathetic situation is in their hands, so I suggest when hiring and firing, scrutinize the situation aggressively before taking any decision. Also, reconsider placing your future in the hands of self-centered people.

> *"I am thankful for all those difficult people in my life. They have shown me exactly who I do not want to be."*

3) Death of a salesman

It was the middle of the night, and after a very exhausting day, I was sound asleep. Suddenly, the mobile rang and I felt quite anxious as I picked it up.

The voice on the other side was so shaky and weary that it was impossible to make out who was on the line. Finally, I heard the familiar tone of a family friend who had been very close to us since childhood.

"I am going to my uncle's place in Australia and I am not sure when I will be back."

"What happened? You seem quite disturbed," I managed to ask during the strange conversation.

"Quite a long story. Will tell you once I am a little comfortable. Right now, it is quite an overwhelming situation."

Well, the promise to call back took three months to materialize. Finally, things were clear, but pretty uncomfortable.

The friend of mine had been working as Vice President of sales in a well-established real estate company. He was doing extremely well and was the most confident person I had ever come across. Despite many hurdles, he had managed to steer clear of any kind of overwhelming challenges.

Although from the outside he managed to present a confident and noteworthy stature, he was gradually dying inside. He had been working unabashedly for more than 18 hours a day, managing his home as well as the professional front. In the process, he had become like a robot, just performing like a machine. His seniors wanted results no matter the situation, which was practically impossible, and in the process, there was a lot of manipulation and fake sales on all fronts. His ethics were long dead.

The euphoria of sales had been replaced by a frenzy to increase the sales figures by hook or by crook. But one fine day, a furious, unsatisfied buyer broke the camel's back. One of the sales executives had sold a 2BHK flat to an investor as a 3BHK, and with all the wrong commitments. The buyer had struck the deal, considering it a lucrative one, but had realized the manipulation after he made the payment. The sales executive had joined the company only a few days ago and struck not one but 3 such deals just to increase his sales figures.

Despite his repeated requests to the directors to arrange elaborate training sessions for the sales department, they were adamant on not wasting any funds on the same. His subordinates had played politics with him for a long time and were quite happy watching his desperate situation. The situation had become so critical that the manipulated buyers had barged into his office and treated him like a murderer. They had humiliated him to the extent that he lost all his zeal and enthusiasm. He just wanted to run away somewhere and hide till his scars were healed.

But finally, it was the death of a salesman. Although my friend was physically alive, he could no longer think of sales as a career and started a new journey in another company and in an alien department.

ANOTHER DEATH OF A SALESMAN.

SOLUTION

There should be an honest and transparent ambience in sales. Rather than fleecing customers and hiding details, the focus should be on retaining the purity of sales.

Figures matter, but should not be given so much priority that employees resort to hideous means to attain them.

The reputation of the company should be maintained and any kind of malpractice should be avoided. Sales leaders need to be kind and understanding toward their sales team, and if they are not able to reach the desired target, then the leaders should be supportive rather than insulting.

"You can be the most productive and most effective, but politics show up as ego, jealousy and sabotage from bosses who can't perform."

— Richie Norton

Managing Sales Ethics

- Follow the leader
- Leader selection is important
- Establish a code of ethics
- Create ethical structures
- Encourage whistle-blowing
- Create an ethical sales climate
- Establish control systems

9

WHY SHOULD SALES
TRAINING BE MANDATORY?

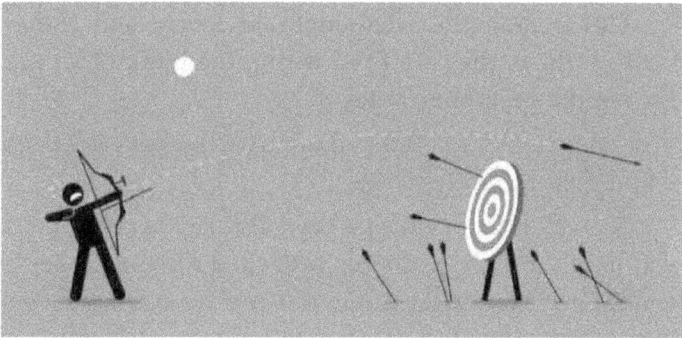

In my vast and widespread experience in sales, I had to deal with multiple sales executives and sales managers. There were quite a lot of eye-opening interactions and tales. But a few of them really made me stand up and pensively consider the discrepancies in sales culture.

A series of random calls from the clients in one of his companies were more complaints than enquiries or conversions. They literally requested him to stop the barge of calls from the salespeople which were more like mental harassment.

What in the world is happening?

As he delved deeper, he heard about similar instances from other companies, too. Sometimes, the buyers were given fake commitments and sold products or services without even thinking about the outcome. The sales employees were only concerned about figures and targets, but in the mad race, they committed blunders.

This made me realize that there was no such system of sales training being offered to salespeople which would have helped them in achieving results without adopting such kinds of harassment. Sales has to be pure and strategic, and there is no place for inexperienced, untrained employees forcing sales down the throats of clients.

Companies hire salespeople randomly, and if they don't perform, they are fired within the blink of an eye. But are they the ones at fault?

Most sales employees simply don't have the skills necessary to lead their teams to success.

So why is there a such a large disparity between those who have the right leadership skills, and those who don't? Frankly, it comes down to the fact that no one has taught them how to be effective coaches, improve sales processes, or recruit the best salespeople.

WHAT SKILLS DO MANY SALES LEADERS LACK?

Sales leaders are normally expected to just perform and give results, but in the process, a basic skill they either lose or don't grasp is time management. They are so occupied generating revenue that they don't train or coach their team on even the basics. Most sales leaders lack the most important characteristic: empathy.

They just become so stone-hearted or callous that they fail to see the stress written on their team's faces. They expect a fresher to become a sales honcho in a day without any proper training or guidance. They hammer for sales, and in turn get hammered by top management. Another shortcoming of most leaders is distrust. If a sales executive fails to perform, the leaders fire or harass them based on the judgments given to them by others.

THE RIGHT SKILLS FOR THE RIGHT SALES – BUT HOW?

Quite simply, those in sales management need to understand that there are areas in which they lack competence – and that they must seek to remedy them through appropriate sales leadership training.

However, it is important to note that not all sales training is created equal. While many touch on how to create a winning process and execute a sales strategy, they rarely cover elements such as mindset and hidden strengths and weaknesses, and, most importantly, don't offer follow-up support after the initial program.

SOLUTION

Each and every human being has different skillsets, so don't try to compare one employee with another. Find and understand the qualities of each salesperson and hone them so they perform their best in whatever they are meant for.

> "It is not your customer's job to remember you. It is your obligation and responsibility to make sure they don't have the chance to forget you."
>
> – Patricia Fripp

EVIDENCE OF MANIPULATION

ARTICLE PUBLISHED IN DU BEAT

The COVID 19 pandemic came as one of the greatest blows to education in modern history. It shut down schools, left millions of students stranded and forced them into child labour and marriage. But for one industry, educational technology, the closing of classroom doors was exactly what cleared their path toward monumental success.

Byju's, the most successful of these ed-tech start-up's, has been valued at USD 18 billion, more than the entire education budget of India for 2021-22. It has acquired other education brands like JEE and NEET coaching giant Aakash Institute, WhiteHat Jr., a company that claims to teach kids as young as 6 to code and skill-development app, Great Learning. It has even gone international, buying up Epic! Osmo and other American education companies.

Fueling its meteoric growth are huge investors like Edelweiss and the Chan Zuckerberg Initiative as well as a host of unethical practises that swindle students and parents out of their money by making misleading claims and false promises. And Byju's is certainly not unique, most other ed-tech platforms have adopted similar strategies for profit.

Byju's incessant flashy ads starring Shah Rukh Khan and WhiteHat Jr.'s promises to turn kids into computer geniuses who create apps worth billions at age 12 might be egregiously false and very irritating, but they're far from their most outrageous techniques for selling their services.

TOXIC WORK CULTURES

Byju's employees are reportedly made to work more than 12 hours a day, skipping meals and rushing from one potential client to another to meet their weekly target of INR 2,00,00 per week. They target everyone from 6th-graders who say they want to become doctors to 12th-graders struggling with competitive exams

(and, of course, their parents) and convince them that they will never be able to succeed without Byju's or one of the companies it owns.

To do this, they partner with schools to push their courses among students, prey on parents' insecurities by asking their children questions that are too advanced for them and convince parents in smaller towns that local coaching institutes will be utterly inadequate in preparing their children for national-level exams.

Even student interns hired by the company aren't spared. They are asked to push the service onto their peers and convince them to first sign up for a free trial and then buy the courses. They often receive calls from frustrated and angry parents who are tired of Byju's insistent marketing.

> *"The primary aim of business is not to earn profit but to serve people--the customers and society at large--to fulfil their needs!"*
>
> —Dr. Vivencio Ballano

10

WHY IS SALES
THE LIFELINE OF AN
ORGANIZATION?

Sales is the heart of an organization, and no business can survive without sales. Sales generate revenue, which is the lifeline of a business.

HOW CAN YOU UNDERESTIMATE AND IGNORE SALES, THEN?

One of the main reasons for the failure of an organization is their negligence of this department. Well-trained and nurtured salespeople can generate the funds that allow a company to function and take it to the heights of success.

No matter how good your operation is, how razor-sharp your technology is, how well-planned your financial goals are, or how progressive and visionary your management techniques are, you must still have a fantastic sales system in place, or everything else is futile.

According to my opinion, sales was and always will be the lifeline of every business.

For a deeper understanding, you need to consider the perspective.

Cash flow is the reason of survival, and this is the blunt truth.

And cash comes from sales. So, from the top to the bottom of an organization, everything is focused on the revenue being generated from the functioning of the sales department. Day in and day out, the pressure flows through the system which is the heart of an organization.

So the basic concept of the survival of a business is solely based on the sales department. Organizations spend oodles of funds on marketing, but it is ultimately synergized through this department, so it is and should be the lifeline of an organization.

Every vision is seen through the eyes of sales procrastinations.

Before laying the first stone of a company or business, the founders and directors envision and procrastinate the sales figures. They only take the first step if the figures are favorable.

Almost all business planning begins and ends with the budgeting process, and all budgets originate and are derived from the sales forecast.

In real estate companies, even before the launch of the project, the senior management has a preview of how many flats or bungalows or offices can be sold to achieve a breakeven point. Only after a near-confirmed sales map is ready do they start the construction work.

Therefore, it is not difficult to say that sales are responsible for the beginning and end of an organization or small or large business.

Sales: the nerve center.

The wiring of every department is ultimately connected to the nerve center that is sales. All the employees besides those functioning in sales are there to make the process easier and more comfortable.

The salaries and other funds depend on the inflow from the sales revenue, so ultimately everything boils down to the nerve center, which has to be optimal to take up the pressure and perform smoothly.

PRODUCTS AS PER THE REQUIREMENTS OF BUYERS

Sales figures are the benchmark for calculating the success or failure of a product, service, or organization. No sales mean that something is wrong. Either your product or service does not meet a need, your marketing is not promoting the product/service correctly, or the sales process should be adjusted. The list is endless.

The directors, business owners, and entrepreneurs will always have their own perspective of sales. If you look around in every city of India and even globally, you will come across such family-owned businesses and companies which are centuries old, but still going strong. The fundamentals behind their survival and growth are their quality standards and service, as well as the pricing which they have maintained over the years. One thing almost all of them have in common is happy employees who get regular perks and motivation as well as security and comfort, which keeps them attached to the company for decades.

There will be a difference of opinions regarding the level of importance sales has in a business and how much emphasis there should be on it. Business owners will also constantly strive to make sure things are even in their company. Whether you see sales as the superstars of growth or just a regular part of business, there is no denying the importance sales has on your business and ultimately your life.

I can, however, confidently point out that flourishing businesses are those that have satisfied, motivated, and secure salespeople. They have strong personal relationships with key customers, or they learn how to build them.

CONCLUSION

Sales was, and will always be, the cash flow department of every organization. So, the more importance and support we give to the sales employees, the more funds generated. This will ensure the sustainability of an organization. Support, security, and comfort as well as financial stability should be ensured for every salesperson to motivate them to become better performers and be loyal to the company.

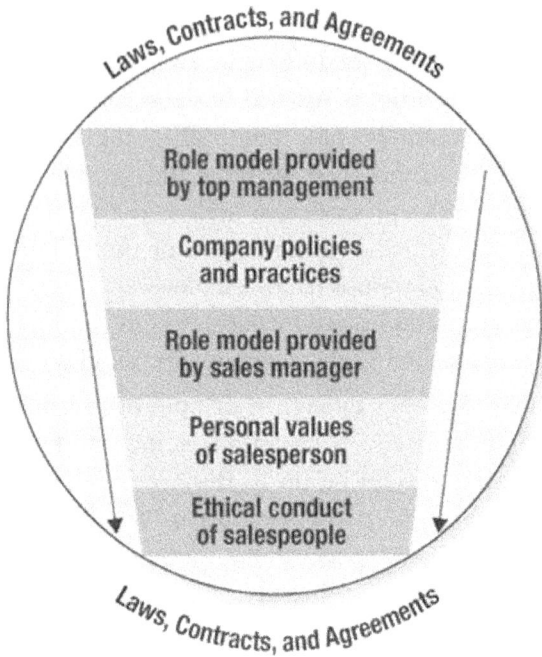

Laws, Contracts, and Agreements

Role model provided
by top management

Company policies
and practices

Role model provided
by sales manager

Personal values
of salesperson

Ethical conduct
of salespeople

Laws, Contracts, and Agreements

*"Most people think 'selling' is the same as 'talking'.
But the most effective salespeople know that listening is
the most important part of their job."*

– Roy Bartell

"The harder the conflict, the more glorious the triumph."

– Thomas Paine

*"Sales are contingent upon the attitude of the salesman,
not the attitude of the prospect."*

– William Clement Stone

11

PURITY OF SALES WITHOUT MANIPULATION

Before we talk about pasteurization and restoring of the purity of sales, we need to understand the discrepancies which need to be worked on.

Some examples of manipulative practices include:

Giving an impression of false urgency and trying to brainwash clients into buying a product or service. Most coaching classes resort to such practices.

Preying on the doubts and ignorance of clients or customers and handing them products which they don't need or will regret buying.

Hiding the facts, especially in services related to educational products and properties.

Forcing a customer beyond his will by harassing him is, again, manipulation. There are many purer ways of selling rather than adhering to unethical practices. The client should never be treated like a bundle of currency.

Such hideous practices may lead to a one-time sale, but for long-term sustainability, the focus should be on maintaining ethical and transparent relationships with customers and clients.

Even though some customers hate random sales calls, they are still just treated like sales leads, only to be exploited for conversions. Such type of practices needs to be avoided to retain the purity of sales.

TRY INNOVATIVE STRATEGIES, NOT CHEATING

Nowadays, most sales strategies are based on productivity by hook or by crook, which is one of the most destructive methods. There are different ways to market products, so you don't have to be manipulative or a cheater. While your goal is still to make a sale, you can respect the customers and clients by presenting a transparent picture and allow them to take their own decisions.

TARGETING THE PERFECT CUSTOMER

If you offer what the right target audience needs or wants, and find ways to connect with them, you don't have to trick them into buying. They'll want to buy what you have.

Develop leads through detailed research and through your current satisfied clients and customers. You don't have to run after buyers; they will come to you if your strategies are systematic and lucrative.

BRANDING THROUGH CUSTOMERS

One satisfied client or customer can be your brand ambassador for a lifetime, so instead of focusing on short-term benefits, focus on word-of-mouth publicity. The consumers who appreciate your services will publicize your business if you value their happiness effectively.

Salespeople who are honest and transparent win more clients than those who hide facts, because the customers value authenticity.

Don't expect deals the moment you interact with a client; instead, offer them detailed knowledge and characteristics of your product. In olden days, salesmen used to simply have long conversations with customers, and in the process sell half their products very deftly. They never used to force any client or customer to just think of buying. In a world with social media, techniques like blog posts and interesting videos can be effectively utilized to impress customers.

Following these strategies can get you connected to the right clients and customers that would benefit from your product without any sign of buyer's remorse or guilt on your end.

SOLUTION

Don't resort to playing with the minds of people; rather, be communicative and understand the needs of each individual buyer. Work from the heart and see the desired results. Buyers are loyal to those who cater to their needs perfectly.

OVEROMING PROFESSIONAL FAILURES

THE STRUGGLES OF STRUGGLES

Although this may seem really outrageous, the hardships of your struggles, or the struggles of your struggles, can be the best teachers of your life.

YOUR DOOMS, YOUR TEACHERS

On encountering a personal or professional failure, the first thought which crosses any person's mind is:

"Oh, God! Why did this happen to me? I have lost everything!"

But if you really look hard around you, then almost every person or business has faced failure at some point or another in their life. Failure has not spared even the toughest and the richest. But did they consider it the end of the road?

The answer is of course not – otherwise they would not have become what they are.

In 2019, Ruchi Soya was heavily under debt and a loss-making unit when Patanjali Ayurveda acquired it for ₹4,350 crores through IBC proceedings. Today, its shares are trading at ₹938 compared to around ₹220 two years ago. The company has given a return of 400% to its investors in two years and has become a profitable entity.

Baba Ramdev looked through the mistakes and reinvented it. So, failures are the best teachers. Learn from them rather than cribbing and losing hope.

NAME IT A STRUGGLE

Normally, when any startup or business fails, the first reaction is that it has failed, while no one considers it a struggle of the struggles. When a child starts learning how to walk, he falls many times but still tries to get up. Do the parents tell him that he has failed? No.

Then why, in a profession or business, do we consider it a failure if it is facing a crunch? Rather, it should be given the name of a "struggle" and instead of crying over spilt milk, we should get up and move on with renewed energy.

"Establishing trust is better than any sales technique."
– Mike Puglia

PLAN THE NEXT STRATEGY

Never blame others for your failures or mistakes. Rather, own them and move on to the next step. The more you reflect on the reasons, the more precious time you lose, and it will become like a whirlpool of emotions from which you can never come out.

Be reflective and pensive and try to understand what triggered the failures.

Once you face your mistakes head-on, rectify them, and plan your next strategies, life will give you a second chance to succeed.

"Once you replace negative thoughts with positive ones, you'll start having positive results."
– Willie Nelson

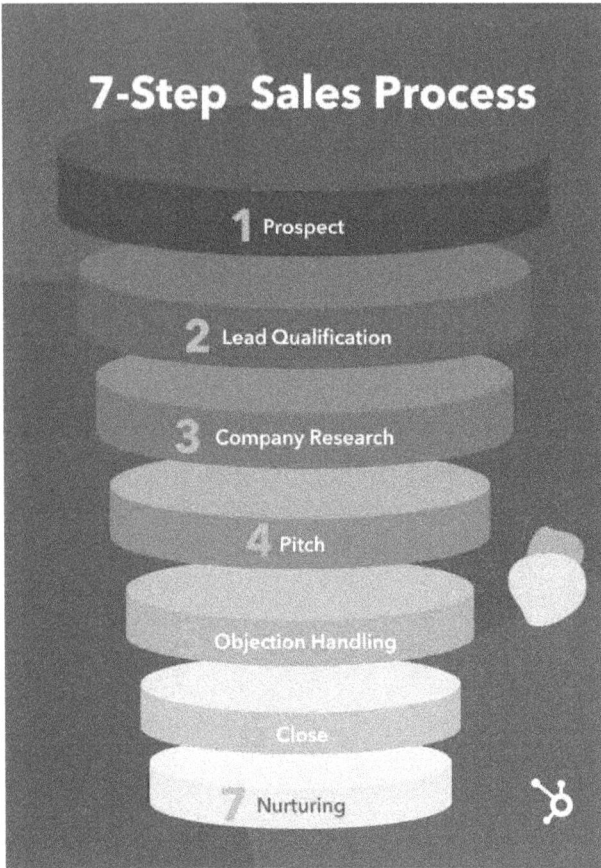

7-Step Sales Process

1 Prospect

2 Lead Qualification

3 Company Research

4 Pitch

Objection Handling

Close

7 Nurturing

12

THE REDEMPTION
OF SALES

In the preceding chapters, we had a lot of discussion regarding the discrepancies in sales and their solutions. The purpose and vision of this book is not just highlighting the problems surrounding sales, but also to iron the loose ends.

I am here to offer strategic remedies for all the dangers engulfing sales and procedures for the same.

The toxic atmosphere in companies and various organizations has become quite claustrophobic, and they need a breath of fresh air. So here I am with some much-needed oxygen.

Sales is an integral and indispensable department of every organization, and the sales employees need to be treated like human beings and not robots.

Even in games like cricket, there are sports psychologists who take care of the stress and other baggage which the players carry. Their duty is to keep them motivated and stress-free so that the players can perform their best during cricket matches. But why only sports the need of the hour is to hire Happiness officer for employees undergoing stressful duties so that they can focus on increasing revenue rather than quitting or lapsing as patients in a hospital.

EFFECTS OF STRESS ON EMPLOYEE PERFORMANCE

Employee stress is a consistent challenge for organizations, as stress contributes to:

Decreased organizational performance

Decreased overall employee performance

Higher ratio of mistakes

Abhorrent work standards

Employees vanishing without any trace

Frequent absences from the office

STRATEGIES FOR INTRODUCING POSITIVITY TO SALES

You might laugh or scorn, but hiring a happiness officer is the best solution for increasing and multiplying sales.

We are shouting from the rooftops about mental health. It applies to employees as well, and especially to those reeling under stress. If you randomly check the blood pressure and stress-related issues of any sales employee, you will find him suffering, without fail.

So, the first thing which companies need to do is recruit a happiness officer who can tackle these issues, and this will gradually support growth of revenue.

The purpose of hiring a Chief Happiness Officer is:

A Chief Happiness Officer is a professional who is **responsible for the happiness of employees in a**

company. He is in charge of interacting with the employees and organizing programs that can go a long way toward improving employee satisfaction, motivation, and abolition of negativity.

The role of a Chief Happiness Officer (CHO) is very important in every company, because it has been proved with many surveys that happier employees are the most resourceful and successful employees. Employee satisfaction is one of the main and most rewarding ways to increase productivity.

GIVE IMPORTANCE TO TRANSPARENT COMMUNICATION.

In our home, we encourage honesty and transparency between family members so that there is bonding between everyone. So why not in the office, too?

Salespeople should not be considered liabilities, but assets.

Offer mental and physical health benefits.

The physical and mental health of the sales team is very crucial for their success.

Organize meditation camps.

Give paid leaves to encourage empathy and enthusiasm.

Encourage employees to take breaks to avoid burnout.

Take the team out on professional tours.

Bring more liveliness into the office.

Be considerate and work out flexible work schedules.

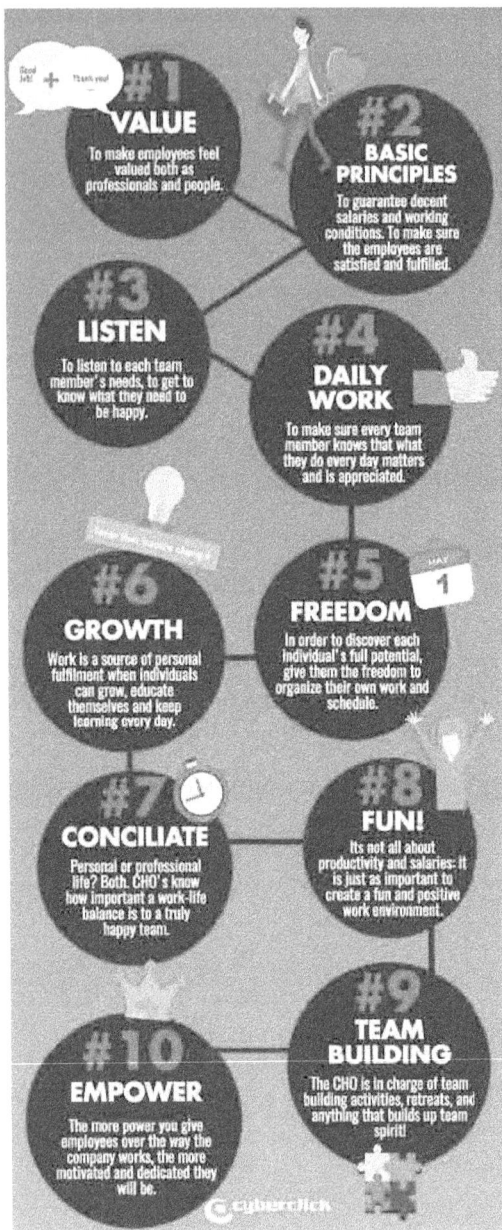

#1 VALUE
To make employees feel valued both as professionals and people.

#2 BASIC PRINCIPLES
To guarantee decent salaries and working conditions. To make sure the employees are satisfied and fulfilled.

#3 LISTEN
To listen to each team member's needs, to get to know what they need to be happy.

#4 DAILY WORK
To make sure every team member knows that what they do every day matters and is appreciated.

#6 GROWTH
Work is a source of personal fulfilment when individuals can grow, educate themselves and keep learning every day.

#5 FREEDOM
In order to discover each individual's full potential, give them the freedom to organize their own work and schedule.

#7 CONCILIATE
Personal or professional life? Both. CHO's know how important a work-life balance is to a truly happy team.

#8 FUN!
Its not all about productivity and salaries: it is just as important to create a fun and positive work environment.

#10 EMPOWER
The more power you give employees over the way the company works, the more motivated and dedicated they will be.

#9 TEAM BUILDING
The CHO is in charge of team building activities, retreats, and anything that builds up team spirit!

cyberclick

13

SALES EMPOWERMENT

Empowerment is a small word, but it is packs a powerful punch.

What exactly is sales empowerment?

Let me explain with an example of an incident from my own personal experience. In one of my previous companies where I was handling a team of sales employees, I encountered numerous hurdles. But one ultimately made me sit back and seriously think about empowerment.

One of my sales executives was handling a very positive prospect and was about to close the deal. The client wanted some extra discount and benefits before handing over the token payment.

The sales executive came to my cabin and asked me for the same, but unfortunately, I had no power or authority over that. I felt quite embarrassed and literally felt like banging my head. Ultimately, the deal got cancelled and we lost a precious sale.

I tried to contact my seniors, but, alas, none of them were available to handle the situation. I realized that although I was the sales head, I was nothing in the eyes of the employees. They were disappointed and very much pessimistic, too. This was a typical situation where I felt that sales empowerment was the most crucial requirement.

THE EXACT DEFINITION OF SALES EMPOWERMENT

Let us go back in history and look at some of the battles which were fought. The leader in charge of the battle used to have many warriors, so in order to win, he used to delegate responsibilities. Those who used to take charge under him as joint leaders or sub-leaders were solely responsible for their team. They had the complete authority to take decisions in order to win the battle and simultaneously safeguard their team.

This teaches us a very important lesson that whether it is a war or an organization, giving authority to team members is the key to success. When someone is empowered, they have the ability to accomplish something, giving them the confidence needed to succeed.

Empowerment of employees is like a strategic management of the key decision makers. All the responsible members should assign the authority and powers clearly along with the risk factors involved. There should be mutual trust and teamwork.

Training of the employees plays a major factor in taking decisions.

ADVANTAGES OF EMPOWERMENT

The best advantage of employee empowerment is loyalty, which leads to less cases of resignations and removes toxicity. The feeling and euphoria of power and authority raises motivation and a duty toward performance.

OPTIMISTIC EMPLOYEES

It has been observed that empowering employees definitely results in an optimistic makeover of the behavior pattern. The employees are focused on creating strategies for sales improvement and don't waste their time and energy on futile matters. The overall scenario transforms into an optimistic system. Just try to delegate responsibilities and give authority to the leaders and managers, and see the change for yourself. Even the smallest employee down the line will be found doing hard work with renewed energy. This is the power of sales empowerment, and any kind of empowerment, in fact.

FAITH IN AUTHORITY

Leaders who empower their team members encourage dedication, a sense of responsibility, and increased performance. The same is true for employees who have been empowered. They have trust in their leader and never challenge his decisions. This leads to harmony in the professional ambience and healthy competition with other organizations. Targets are achieved without manipulation of figures, and there is remarkable growth in the revenue and image of the organization.

HEIGHTENED PLANNING AND DELIVERANCE

Many times, I have found even managers who are capable of deliverance failing to perform. In most cases, feelings of dejection and pessimism demotivate them. They have to get permission for each and every decision from their seniors and feel like their team members don't respect them the way they should. Some employees even cross the hierarchy and try to be closer to the leaders who have the authority.

A manager without power is useless.

How would you feel if your team member ridiculed you?

So instead of blaming the managers or the sales leader, try to instil employee empowerment fundamentals in the organization. It will surely lead to heightened planning and deliverance.

ETHICAL PERFORMERS

WHY DO EMPLOYEES RESORT TO MANIPULATION IN SALES?

The answer is very simple. They don't have the enthusiasm and energy to give results with proper planning. Most of their brainwork is focused on the negativity and lack of authority.

They feel that if their seniors can't take any decisions, then it is useless to focus on hard work, and this pessimism results in manipulation and unethical practices being used to achieve targets. They vent out their frustrations either on the team members or the clients, which leads to further friction.

CONCLUSION :

Treat your employees as your family, and transfer authority to responsible people so that there is no loss of business. Don't expect the leaders to trust you if you can't trust them. Loyalty and trust are bred from faith, and this is true in both personal and professional scenarios. In 99% of cases, you will find employee empowerment will never result in a breach of trust; rather, it will boost growth and employee satisfaction.

14

SIGNIFICANCE OF THE HR DEPARTMENT IN SALES PRODUCTIVITY

A) Extensive knowledge of products

The HR department is just not for recruitment. They must understand the company's products and the sales strategies used in marketing them. This will allow them to understand what talent is needed and in what places to find candidates. There should be coordination between HR and the sales leaders so they can hire the best sales talent.

The vision of the sales leader should be in the minds of the HR. Before hiring anyone, they should provide complete clarity to the salesperson. This includes subjects like the products that are best for sales generation, the types of sales strategies that are needed, expected sales productivity, and the importance of focusing on ethical sales.

B) Recognize the different sales roles

The HR department must recognize all the different sales roles within the sales department. There are many subroles in sales that involve identifying sales leads, collecting data, calling the prospective buyers and investors, etc. The assigning of duties should be done very tactically so that the right person is doing the right job. This will ultimately lead to sales growth.

They must emphasize differentiating each role when recruiting new employees. Sometimes, if an amateur tele-caller is assigned to dealing with investors or buyers, he or she may become a failure. Many salespeople do not perform because they were put in the wrong position. If the HR department better understood their skills, the employee's productivity would have increased.

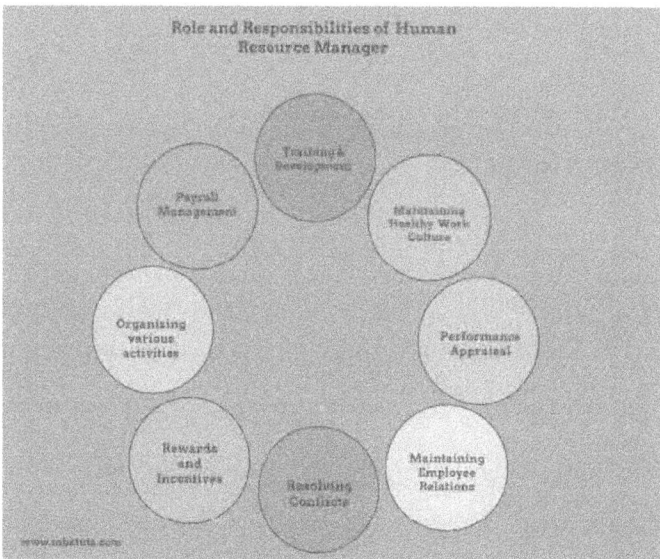

C) Clarity of the recruitment requirements

Human resources are sometimes under too much stress or in too much of a hurry to hire sales employees that they just focus on hiring people, rather than giving importance to the candidates having the right skills. Rather, they should interact closely with the sales leader or the seniors to understand the qualities they are looking for in prospective employees.

Since the sales department is frequently looking for skilled salespeople, HR should focus on conducting interviews for skilled people who are interested in joining in the near future.

Also, there should be a fixed standard skillset required so that the existing sales employees can also be trained to meet those standards and deliver the required performance. Hiring should not be done just to fill the position. Sales growth and retention should also be given equal importance so that talented people do not leave and are given the required importance.

D) Perform screening on candidates

An experienced HR team has the systems and strategies to conduct verification and background checks on the applicants. They can determine whether all the details in a resume are true and whether the candidate's achievements are genuine. There should be a minimum of two to three interview rounds for shortlisting the candidates so that only the eligible ones will pass the interviews.

E) Provide training for average sales performers

Sales heads or leaders focus more on the top performers and train the weakest ones. But their attention is not on the average performers who have the capability to do better if they are trained properly. There should be balanced attention and training imparted to every type of salesperson so that they can overcome their weaknesses. Therefore, the HR department has a key role in organizing such programs for them to participate in and learn specialized sales techniques from.

This will allow them to grow to a superior level. For example, they can organize motivational seminars and training programs. They can also hold meetings to educate the staff in the sales department on how to use various resources.

HR can also research the best methods and find the best sales trainers who can boost the morale of the salespeople. Providing systematic training can build the perfect candidates and boost employee retention. Training videos of the best sales trainers and coaches can reduce the training costs, too.

F) Be supportive of the sales team

The best way HR can reduce stress amongst salespeople is to proactively listen to whatever is troubling them. It can be very mundane to work in a stressful environment, so the salespeople definitely need supportive people who can understand their woes. They can also organize motivational sessions to boost the morale of the employees. HR should provide support for all groups of employees, not just those who aren't performing well.

G) Strategic and fulfilling incentive plans

There should be incentive plans to motivate salespeople during the entire year, not just during festivals. This is quite crucial to boost their energy and fuel their desire to earn more. Human resources should collaborate with the sales department to develop such plans. The sales manager should involve the HR department regarding the incentives they want to offer the sales team so that HR can inform the team. A compensation plan can motivate the sales team to maintain a good performance and meet the company goals. The sales executives can be rewarded appropriately so that they are not concerned about their low salaries. In this way, the company can retain top performers and productive salespeople.

H) Keep an eye on employee performance

Almost all the time, many salespeople suffer from being overworked. If they keep working in such circumstances, their productivity level will drop. If HR and the sales team keep an eye out for such incidents, then they can fix the situation and ensure that these employees don't get over-exhausted and lose their desire to work. A one-on-one session can be of great help, and if required, some recreational activities should be conducted to reduce stress levels.

I) A welcoming ambience

The HR department can create a welcoming ambience for new joiners so that they can learn the system and become a part of the sales team. HR can create orientation programs for new workers to learn more about the office environment and their job roles. They can make the first few days of the job special to help the new employees adapt to their work.

The HR department should plan such programs for new salespeople to raise their energy levels. After orientation, HR should monitor their progress to see how well the new workers are adapting to their workplace.

SPECIALIZED PERSONALITY TESTING

In some companies, the recruitment process involves personality testing to establish the assignment of responsibilities which are perfectly suited to the candidates' attributes. Personality tests can reveal the interests and skills of the candidates. It can also reveal their personality styles. Such tests can go a long way toward increasing the performance of the candidates.

For example, a person who has excellent communication skills could be an excellent tele-caller rather than working as an assistant to a manager.

J) Create a multi-faceted sales force

HR plays an important role in recruiting a sales team which can deal with different types of customers. A multi-faceted sales force is especially important when the customers come with a variety of requirements.

A multi-talented team can introduce different sales ideas, and people from varied backgrounds can offer their unique perspectives. This will help build a positive image of the brand and motivate the best sales performers to work for the company.

K) Zero revenge scenario and excellent policies for outgoing employees

After suffering from deluges of insults and frustrations, people may frequently feel a desire to take revenge. After all, how much torture can an employee take, day in and day out?

Here, the seniors and HR play a key role by hiring peace managers or corporate coaches who can listen to the woes of the tortured and frustrated but skilled people. Rather than regretting the loss of trained sales staff, such events should be mitigated by introducing them to coaches or counsellors.

They are experts in diverting the attention of such devastated employees looking for revenge. Their mindset can be altered to be more positive and they can be convinced to not resort to negative tactics.

The same is true for those who have given notice or are on the verge of resigning due to frustration. Even one such negative employee can bring about a cascade of negativity and lead to the company's downfall. When such an employee goes to a competitor or any other organization, they are bound to vent out their experiences, which can be quite demeaning.

So before they leave, the utmost importance should be placed on retaining them or having a very positive farewell so that they leave all the negativity behind and make a fresh start with a positive image of the organization.

15

CONCLUSION

THE EVERGREEN SALES MANTRA

"Once you replace negative thoughts with positive ones, you'll start having positive results."

– Willie Nelson

So, friends, I hope my thoughts and solutions on avoiding failures and spearheading success for sales and salespeople have been helpful.

My ultimate aim in writing this book is to bring back the pious form of sales culture. I hope this book is helpful to salespeople and organizations around the globe. Just read and follow the solutions provided within, and I am sure your entire perspective will change and your sales will grow.

Carve a niche for yourself and become a sales expert without compromising on quality.

Understand the thought processes of your salespeople, because they are the ones who will take your company to new heights of success and revenue.

Regards and best wishes,
Dr. Prannay G. Sharma